# JUNIOR BIOGRAPHIES

WITHDRAWN FROM WORTH LIBRARY

Rebecca Kraft Rector

# SHAWN MENDES

## SINGER-SONGWRITER

**Enslow Publishing**
101 W. 23rd Street
Suite 240
New York, NY 10011
USA

enslow.com

# WORDS TO KNOW

**chaperone**  To have an adult present to be sure young people behave properly.

**contemporary**  Happening now, modern.

**cover**  A new recording of someone else's song.

**debut**  To appear for the first time.

**descent**  Family background.

**EP**  Extended play record.

**hashtag**  A word or phrase used on social media to tell what a message is about.

**influential**  Having power to affect others.

**platinum**  A distinction given to albums that sell at least one million copies.

**single**  A recording of one song.

# CONTENTS

Shawn Mendes

Shawn Mendes is a superstar singer and songwriter. But before he hit it big, he was an ordinary boy next door.

## FAMILY AND SCHOOL

Shawn Peter Raul Mendes was born on August 8, 1998. He is Canadian. He grew up in the small town of Pickering, Ontario. His parents are Karen and Manuel. Karen is English. Manuel is of Portuguese descent. Aaliyah is Shawn's sister. She is five years younger than Shawn.

In school, Shawn had average grades and good friends. He played soccer and ice hockey. He took acting lessons

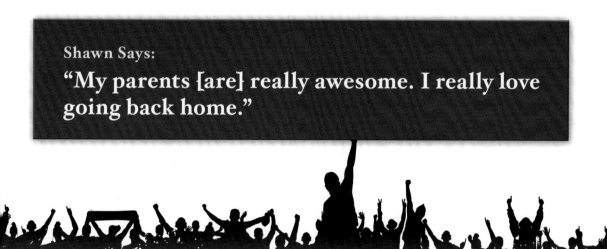

Shawn Says:
**"My parents [are] really awesome. I really love going back home."**

Shawn grew up in Pickering, Ontario. The city is located on Lake Ontario.

and loved being in the spotlight. He was also in the glee club and played piano.

## LEARNING TO SING AND PLAY

When Shawn was fourteen, he taught himself to play the guitar. He learned by watching YouTube videos. He practiced for hours. The first song he learned was "Soul Sister" by Train. He also studied online singers and tried to copy them.

Soon Shawn began posting his own YouTube videos. He sang and played guitar. He performed covers of popular music. He posted on other social media sites, too.

Shawn thought he was a wizard until he was twelve years old.

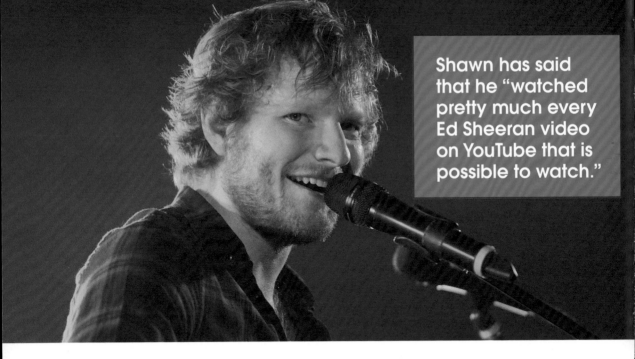

Shawn has said that he "watched pretty much every Ed Sheeran video on YouTube that is possible to watch."

It was a fun thing to do when he was bored. Sometimes kids at school insulted his videos. His friends and family always supported him, though. Shawn admired Ed Sheeran. He is a popular singer and songwriter. He wanted to be like Sheeran. So, he began writing his own songs. He also admired John Mayer's music.

A new video-sharing service started in 2012. It was called Vine. Vine videos could only last six seconds. That was all Shawn needed.

## OVERNIGHT SENSATION

In 2013, Shawn made a new recording. He sang a Justin Bieber song. It was called "As Long as You Love Me." As usual, he recorded in his bedroom. He sang and played his guitar. He posted six seconds on Vine. The next day,

Shawn became famous thanks to Vine, a popular video-sharing app.

he checked it. He wanted to see if anyone had watched. He thought something was wrong with the site. But it was correct. Overnight he'd gained ten thousand likes. He had thousands of followers.

Shawn continued to post new videos. Often he did not wear a shirt. The hashtag #shirtlessshawn became popular. He asked his fans which songs he should sing. The number of his followers soared.

## MAGCON

Shawn performed his first concert in Toronto. It was his first public appearance. He was fifteen years old. In November, he joined the Magcon Tour. Magcon stands for Meet and Greet Convention. Magcon brought social

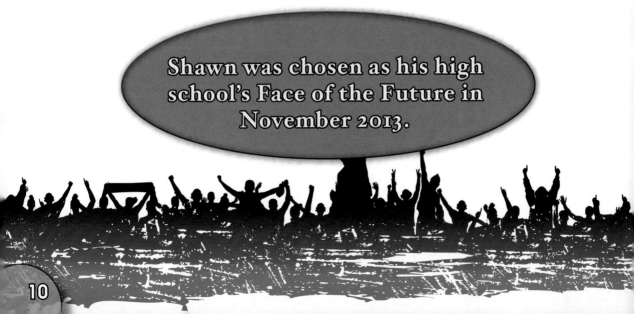

Shawn was chosen as his high school's Face of the Future in November 2013.

Shawn performed for his fans in Toronto in 2014.

Shawn Says:

"My sister recorded, like, the first 50 Vines I ever did. She has to get cred."

media stars together. They toured and met fans. The manager kept everything wholesome. The events were always **chaperoned**. Only a few Magcon stars were singers. Mostly they signed autographs and posed for pictures. The events sold thousands of tickets. They sold out quickly. Shawn was still in school at this time.

In January 2014, Andrew Gertler saw Shawn on YouTube. Gertler was a music manager. He was impressed.

## A RECORD DEAL

Gertler sent the link to Island Records. The record company said Shawn was a superstar! Shawn signed with Island Records in May 2014.

Shawn wrote his first single. It was called "Life of the Party." Island Records put it on iTunes. The song went to number one in forty-five minutes. It was number 24 on *Billboard*'s Hot 100 chart. Shawn was fifteen years, eleven months, and four days old. He was the youngest person to debut that high on the chart.

Shawn took online classes to keep up with school.

Once Shawn got his record deal and first number one hit, he started playing to larger audiences.

## ON THE CHARTS

Soon *The Shawn Mendes EP* was released. It rose to number one on the iTunes charts. It only took forty-five minutes. It also reached number five on the *Billboard* charts. Shawn won the Teen Choice Award for Web Star in Music. He was also named one of *TIME*'s 25 Most Influential Teens for 2014.

In early 2015, Shawn's first studio album came out. *Handwritten* debuted at number one on the charts. "Believe" was one of the songs on the album. The Disney Channel included it on the *Descendants* movie soundtrack.

Shawn accepts his Teen Choice Award on August 16, 2015.

Shawn appears onstage with Taylor Swift in 2015.

Shawn Says:

**"Taylor [Swift] told me that when you get onstage, everyone there just wants to have a good time. It really helped my confidence."**

"Stitches" came out in March. It became his first top ten single on the *Billboard* charts. "Stitches" went triple platinum by the end of the year. In May, Shawn went on tour with superstar Taylor Swift. For the second year in a row, Shawn made *TIME*'s 25 Most Influential Teens list.

# CHAPTER 4
# SUPERSTAR

Shawn made his acting debut in January 2016. He also signed up to do modeling. And, of course, he was still singing.

## TOURING THE WORLD

Shawn had a world tour in 2016. The tour sold out in six minutes. "Treat You Better" was on *Billboard*'s top ten. It went triple platinum. Shawn wrote every song on the album *Illuminate*. The single "Mercy" went double platinum.

Shawn's Illuminate World Tour in 2017 sold out. "There's Nothing Holdin' Me Back" was another top ten single. He had three number one songs on *Billboard*'s

Shawn used Twitter to ask if he could be on the CW show *The 100*. The producer said yes!

Shawn performs for a big crowd on the *Today* show in 2016.

Adult **Contemporary** chart. He was the first to do that before the age of twenty. Shawn was one of *TIME*'s 30 Most Influential Teens of 2017.

Shawn plays his first show on the Illuminate tour in 2017.

## MAKING A DIFFERENCE

Shawn wants to make a difference in the world. He has helped many causes. He created Notes from Shawn. He asked his fans to join him. They wrote positive messages like "You rock." Then they put it on someone's locker. Shawn also worked with Pencils of Promise. He helped raise money to build schools in Ghana, a country in west Africa.

In 2017, Shawn was in Mexico City for a concert.

An earthquake struck the city. Shawn was not hurt. But hundreds of people died. He worked with the Red Cross to raise money. He also gave $100,000 of his own money.

Whether he's singing, writing his own hit songs, or making a difference in the lives of strangers, Shawn is certainly on a roll. Fans everywhere can't wait to see what he will do next.

Shawn signs autographs for his fans. "It's amazing having so many people care so much about what I'm doing," he says.

Shawn Says:

"Show more love. Don't judge every chance you get. It makes you and the person receiving it feel great. A pretty simple way to happiness."

# TIMELINE

**1998** Shawn Peter Raul Mendes is born on August 8.

**2013** Shawn's cover of "As Long as You Love Me" gets ten thousand likes overnight.

**2014** Signs with Island Records at age fifteen.

**2014** Releases debut single, "Life of the Party."

**2015** Releases first studio album, *Handwritten*.

**2015** Tours with Taylor Swift.

**2016** Travels from New York to Asia on Shawn Mendes World Tour.

**2016** Graduates from high school.

**2017** Headlines Illuminate World Tour.

**2017** Earns sixth top 40 hit on *Billboard's* Hot 100.

## BOOKS

Caravantes, Peggy. *Shawn Mendes: Pop Star*. Mankato, MN: Momentum, 2017.

Johnson, Robin. *Shawn Mendes*. New York, NY: Crabtree Publishing, 2018.

Sprinkel, Katy. *Shawn Mendes: Superstar Next Door*. Chicago, IL: Triumph Books, 2016.

Zakarin, Debra Mostow. *Shawn Mendes: It's My Time*. New York, NY: Scholastic, 2016.

## WEBSITES

**Disney Video**

*video.disney.com/watch/believe-official-shawn-mendes-5197500dc9e8aef97e774bb7*
Shawn Mendes performs "Believe" from the *Descendants* soundtrack.

**Oh My Disney**

*ohmy.disney.com/music/2014/08/07/can-you-pass-this-shawn-mendes-trivia-quiz/*
Can you pass this Shawn Mendes trivia quiz?

**Shawn Mendes Official Site**

*shawnmendesofficial.com*
See tour dates, news, videos, and official merchandise.

# INDEX

Published in 2019 by Enslow Publishing, LLC.
101 W. 23rd Street, Suite 240, New York, NY 10011

Copyright © 2019 by Enslow Publishing, LLC.
All rights reserved.

No part of this book may be reproduced by any means without the written permission of the publisher.

**Library of Congress Cataloging-in-Publication Data**
Names: Rector, Rebecca Kraft, author.
Title: Shawn Mendes : singer-songwriter / Rebecca Kraft Rector.
Description: New York : Enslow Publishing, 2019. | Series: Junior biographies | Audience: Grades 3-5| Includes bibliographical references and index.
Identifiers: LCCN 2018010209| ISBN 9781978502062 (library bound) | ISBN 9781978503007 (pbk.) | ISBN 9781978503014 (6 pack)
Subjects: LCSH: Mendes, Shawn, 1998–Juvenile literature. | Singers–Canada–Biography–Juvenile literature.
Classification: LCC ML3930.M444 R43 2019 | DDC 782.42164092 [B] –dc23
LC record available at https://lccn.loc.gov/2018010209

Printed in the United States of America

**To Our Readers:** We have done our best to make sure all website addresses in this book were active and appropriate when we went to press. However, the author and the publisher have no control over and assume no liability for the material available on those websites or on any websites they may link to. Any comments or suggestions can be sent by email to customerservice@enslow.com.

**Photos Credits:** Cover, p. 1 Lester Cohen /Getty Images; pp. 2, 3, 22, 23, 24, back cover (curves graphic) Alena Kazlouskaya/Shutterstock.com; p. 4 Debby Wong/Shutterstock.com; p. 6 igor kisselev/Alamy Stock Photo; p. 8 Dave J Hogan/Getty Images; p. 9 DWDMedia/Alamy Stock Photo; p. 11 Victor Biro/Alamy Stock Photo; p. 14 Andrew Chin/FilmMagic/Getty Images; p. 15 Kevin Winter/Getty Images; p. 16 Suzi Pratt/LP5/Getty Images; p. 19 Charles Sykes/Invision/AP; p. 20 Roberto Ricciuti/Redferns/Getty Images; p. 21 Michael Hurcomb/Corbis Entertainment/Getty Images; interior page bottoms (audience) Amitofo/Shutterstock.com.